D0198416

AN LEABHARLANN
COLÁISTE MHUIRE
INSTITIÚD OIDEACHAIS
MARINO.

BEATRICE HOLLYER has worked as a journalist, writer and newscaster. She began her media career in South Africa before moving to the UK, where she has lived for the past ten years.
Today she works as a freelance writer.
Her first book for Frances Lincoln was
Wake Up World! A Day in the Life of Children Around the World,
which was also published in association with Oxfam.

D019847

For my daughter Clementine, my mother and my grandmother

Let's Eat! Children and their Food Around the World
copyright © Frances Lincoln Limited 2003

Text copyright © Frances Lincoln Limited 2003
All location photographs reproduced by permission of Oxfam GB
copyright © Oxfam GB and individual photographers as named 2003

Photograph of Jamie Oliver and children reproduced by kind permission
of David Loftus. Jamie Oliver recipe reproduced by kind permission of
Penguin Books Limited, 80 Strand, London WC2R 0RL

First published in Great Britain in 2003 by Frances Lincoln Limited,
4 Torriano Mews, Torriano Avenue, London NW5 2RZ

www.franceslincoln.com

First paperback edition 2003

All rights reserved.
No part of this publication may be reproduced, stored in a retrieval
system, or transmitted, in any form, or by any means, electrical,
mechanical, photocopying, recording or otherwise without the
prior written permission of the publisher or a licence permitting
restricted copying. In the United Kingdom such licences are
issued by the Copyright Licensing Agency,
90 Tottenham Court Road, London W1P 9HE.

British Library Cataloguing in Publication Data available on request

ISBN 0-7112-2286-X

Printed in Singapore

9 8 7 6 5 4 3 2 1

Oxfam and the publishers would like to thank all the children who took part in *Let's Eat!*, and their families and communities for their enthusiastic support. Oxfam and the publishers would also like to thank the photographers, who were commissioned by Oxfam to spend time with the five children featured in the book.

Toby Adamson visited St Gervais in South-west France to take photographs of Jordan. Then he flew to Magdalena Town in Mexico to see Luis and his family.

Jim Holmes travelled from his home in Laos to Bangkok, the capital of Thailand, to take photographs of AA.

Shailan Parker went to see Yamini and her family in Kolkata, India.

Paul Weinberg took the photographs of Thembe, at home in her village near Durban, South Africa.

*Oxfam GB will receive a royalty for each copy of this book sold in the UK.
Oxfam is a Registered Charity no. 202918. Oxfam GB is a member of Oxfam International.*

Oxfam works with others to overcome poverty and suffering.

LET'S EAT!

Children and their Food Around the World

BEATRICE HOLLYER

Introduction by JAMIE OLIVER

FRANCES LINCOLN IN ASSOCIATION WITH OXFAM

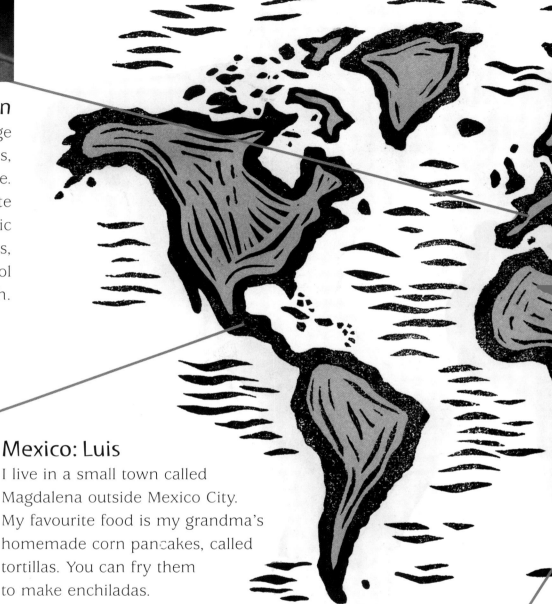

France: Jordan

I live in a village called St Gervais, in the countryside. I have seven favourite foods. I love garlic bread and oysters, but I don't like school dinners much.

Mexico: Luis

I live in a small town called Magdalena outside Mexico City. My favourite food is my grandma's homemade corn pancakes, called tortillas. You can fry them to make enchiladas.

South Africa: Thembe

I live in the hills outside the east coast city of Durban, where it is warm and wet. My favourite food is Weetabix. I also like to chew on pieces of sugar cane.

OF FOOD

Thailand: AA
I live in the middle of busy Bangkok, the capital city. I love eggs so much, I eat them all the time. I don't like red hot chilli peppers!

Contents

India: Yamini
I live in a big city called Kolkata. I have mangoes and watermelon every day in summer. My favourite dish is flat bread filled with potatoes and onion.

I don't know about you, but I've always been really curious about what other people eat. Being nosy is how I've got some of my best ideas as a chef — and discovered some of my favourite things to eat. This book lets you peek into the lives of five children around the world and find out what it's like to be them. If you live in Thailand, do you have to like chilli peppers? Do they eat loads of weird stuff in other countries — or does everyone like popcorn, pancakes and corn on the cob? Do all kids love sweets and ice cream as much as you do?

I love it that everyone has such strong memories of what they ate as children. This book is about those memories happening in kitchens all over the world. Imagine being these kids, try out their recipes. Have loads of fun, like they do, smelling, touching, creating, tasting, laughing and eating. That's what it's all about!

Jamie
x

Jamie's Chocolate Biscuits

140g butter • 140g caster sugar • 2 egg yolks • 255g self-raising flour
30g cocoa powder • 30 squares of chocolate (milk, white or plain)
2 round cookie cutters, one about 4cm wide and the other about 5cm wide

Heat the oven to 190°C / 375°F / Gas Mark 5.

Grease a large baking sheet. Beat the butter and sugar together until pale. Beat in the egg yolks, then the flour and cocoa powder. Turn out the dough, knead it and put it in the fridge for twenty minutes or so.

Sprinkle the work surface with flour then thinly roll out about a third of the dough. Cut out 30 circles with the smaller cutter. Put a square of chocolate in the middle of each one. Roll out the rest of the dough and cut out 30 circles with the bigger cutter. Put one on top of each chocolate square. Press gently all the way around to seal the edges and keep the chocolate in. Bake for 10 minutes and eat hot or cold. Easy peasy, lovely jubbly!

SOUTH AFRICA

Rejoice Thembelihle Mthembu, Thembe for short, is eight years old. She lives with her grandmother, uncle, aunt and three cousins in the green hills outside the city of Durban, on South Africa's east coast. Thembe and her family don't have much money, but they always have plenty to eat because their crops grow easily in the warm, wet climate.

"My favourite food is Weetabix, but I don't get to eat it very often. I like to chew on a piece of umoba (sugar cane)."

Thembe's village has no electricity or running water. Most days, Thembe walks down to the bottom of the valley, where a spring bubbles up through the rock into a pool. She carries the water back up the hill in a clay pot called a calabash.

Thembe begins her day by helping her grandmother, Gogo, make a big bowl of puthu for breakfast. Puthu is a stiff porridge made from maize, which is grown in the fields around the village. Thembe shares the puthu with her uncle, aunt and cousins. Her mother and father live with her father's family in another village. After breakfast, Thembe walks across the hills to school.

"When I grow up, I would like a well-paying job so we can spend less time thinking about food."

At school, Thembe does some weeding in the vegetable garden. The children can take what they grow home to their families, or they sell it to raise money for the school. Thembe thinks working in the garden is important but boring – she would rather be cooking.

After school, Thembe collects some firewood and builds a fire underneath the cooking pot. Sometimes Gogo asks her to climb the lemon or mango tree to pick fruit. Today she needs mealie meal (maize flour) so she asks Thembe to walk to the grocery store.

On the way home, Thembe carries the mealie meal home on her head. If she really concentrates, she can do it without holding on. All the women in Thembe's village carry firewood and water this way.

"I like looking at the crisps and sweets in the shop. Now and then Gogo has some spare change and lets me buy some."

Thembe starts dinner by boiling the mealie meal to make puthu. She knows how to cook most things, and only needs help to prepare a whole meal. Tonight's dinner is her favourite: beef, grilled above the cooking fire, with barbecued mealies (corn cobs), madumbes (a root vegetable like potato), puthu and amasi (sour milk), which they have as a sauce and as a drink on its own.

The puthu is served first to fill them up and make the meat go further. Thembe piles some into a bowl with some vegetables and sits down to share it with her cousins. Children, men and women all eat separately, using their fingers, according to Zulu tradition. As she scoops up the food, Thembe chatters excitedly with her cousins about the big wedding party planned for the next day.

A special day in Thembe's life — a family wedding

Next morning, Thembe helps her aunt Ntombi tie her best skirt and shawl and put on a special head-dress, ready for the wedding. Thembe wishes she was going as well, but she has a large family and her aunt and uncle are going to represent them all.

The bride and groom, who are both related to Thembe, have saved up for a traditional wedding. According to Zulu custom, even if money is short, there must be plenty of food and drink for everyone. Before they leave, the bride's friends pin gifts of money to her head-dress. Then they walk in a procession to the groom's village.

When they arrive, the bride's brother dances and sings a story about their family. He acts it out with sticks and shields made from animal skins.

The children at the wedding think the dancing is the most exciting part of the day. Like Thembe, they love dressing up in beaded head-bands, belts and necklaces.

"There will be Coca Cola and orange fizzy drink at the wedding feast, and a special pudding made with condensed milk. I hope my aunt will bring some back for me."

The groom's friends have killed two cows for the wedding feast. The best pieces are barbecued for the men, and the rest is put into big pots to stew. The meat is served with soft, doughy bread, which is steamed on top of the meat in the pots, and lots of different salads.

After a long day of singing and dancing, the feasting goes on late into the night.

11

MEXICO

Luis Emanuel Sanchez Jimenez is six. His family's pet name for him is Guicho, but his teachers call him Emanuel, which he likes better. He lives in a small town called Magdalena between the countryside and Mexico City. More people live in Mexico City than in any other city in the world.

Magdalena is high up, so the air is fresh and cool. From the church you can look down into the valley. Magdalena was once a farming village. Now most people who live there go to work in the city every day. Luis' father drives them there and back in his bus.

Luis lives in a two-room house with his parents and sister. His grandparents farm a small plot of land nearby. They grow corn and keep sheep and chickens. Luis enjoys collecting eggs and seeing how food grows, but what he likes best is learning to look after the sheep.

When Luis gets up in the morning, he washes his face with water from a big cement basin in the courtyard. Then he has some cold rice pudding, or cornflakes, and chocolate milk. His school has running water so he brushes his teeth there after the morning snack break.

"I have juice and a cake at school, but sometimes I don't eat it because I want to go off quickly and play with my friends."

Luis is too excited to eat his cake today. It is the start of the Christmas holidays and his parents are coming to see him perform in the class nativity play. While Luis waits his turn, he watches his classmates tell the story of 'El Burito de Belen', a small donkey who travels to Bethlehem.

Luis carefully carries his gold paper crown as he leaves school with his mother and his little sister Ana. They are going to have a holiday lunch with his grandparents. On the way, they shop for food. They do this every day as they don't have a fridge at home.

"I am always asking Mum to peel an orange for me. I like to suck the sweet juice out."

Luis and Ana enjoy helping their mother decide what to buy. At the bakery, Luis chooses a cake for after supper. Then they go to the tortilla grinders for some tortillas (corn pancakes). They eat tortillas at nearly every meal. Luis' mother buys them by the kilo, but his grandmother makes her own. Their last stop is the greengrocer's, where they buy some fat cactus leaves for a special salad with coriander and salt.

As soon as Luis arrives at his grandparents' house, he hurries to feed the sheep and herd them into the small pasture. While he helps his grandfather with the animals, his grandmother cooks tortillas on the fire. She makes them with corn she grows herself. Luis thinks her homemade tortillas taste much better than the bought ones he has at home.

A special day in Luis' life — fiesta

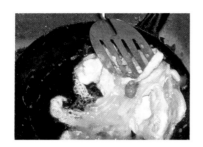

Just before Christmas, Luis visits his other grandparents for a fiesta (festival) to celebrate their town's patron saint. Everyone gets up early for church and fireworks, then they come home for a big family brunch. Luis eats sweet bread, although his mother encourages him to try some omelette, fried beans or fish soup. There are piles of hot tortillas on the table.

**"My favourite food is enchiladas
(fried tortillas) with tuna fish or cheese.
I can eat six of them at one meal!"**

Luis likes to dip his enchiladas in a spicy tomato salsa (sauce) called picadillo. His grandmother makes it with chopped tomatoes, onions, coriander and green chillies. She adds a pinch of salt and a squeeze of lemon juice.

As night falls, Luis' mother and father take him and his sister to the fairground in town. The streets have been decorated with flowers and streamers. People crowd round stalls selling every kind of food and drink. Luis chooses an enchilada from one stall, then an ice cream with fruit from another.

Luis stays up very late to enjoy the fiesta. The best part is the fairground rides, although they whirl him around so fast he's glad his father is holding on to him. He's looking forward to two more days of celebrations and feasting before he goes home to Magdalena for Christmas.

17

THAILAND

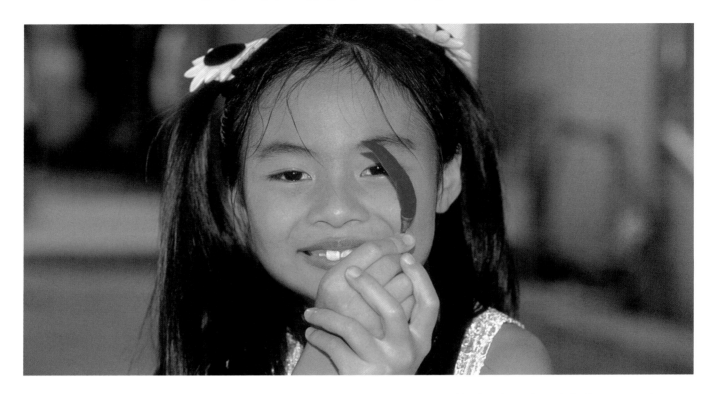

Kamalotas Sudasna lives in Bangkok, the capital city of Thailand, with her mother, father, grandmother and brother. Everyone calls her by her nickname, AA. She is eight and her brother, Sutaspong, is three. AA prefers plain food to traditional spicy Thai dishes. She especially avoids red chili peppers, which are used in cooking to add a fiery flavour.

AA enjoys going to the supermarket with her family to buy rice and other packaged food. Like most people in Bangkok, they buy fish, meat, vegetables and fruit every day at the local market, or from street traders who walk into the city in the early morning.

🐟 AA's grandmother, Khun Yai, does all the cooking for AA's family, including her uncles, aunts and cousins who live in the same building. Today Khun Yai has bought some steamed rice from a street trader on her way back from the market. AA and her cousin have some for breakfast with AA's favourite dish, khai jiow moo supp – Thai fried eggs.

"I love eggs.
I eat them all the time,
at nearly every meal."

🐟 A monk from the nearby temple comes to AA's house every morning. AA feels special when it is her turn to give him the food her grandmother has prepared. Her family are Buddhists, and supporting the monks who study at the temple is an important tradition for them.

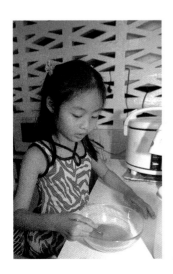

🐟 Sometimes AA cooks her favourite Thai fried eggs herself. She shakes some salty soy sauce into the beaten egg mixture to make it more tasty.

 After school, while her mother and father are still at work in their offices, AA goes to the market with her grandmother to shop for dinner. Khun Yai is teaching AA how to choose the freshest fish, the ones with bright eyes and red gills. They get some pork at the butcher's stall, some quails' eggs, then some greens. AA and Khun Yai take turns to carry the heavy basket.

Back at home, AA is in charge of cooking the quails' eggs for dinner. While her father builds up the fire in a small charcoal stove in the courtyard, AA puts oil in the holes of a special egg pan so that the eggs won't stick. Then she breaks a quail's egg into each hole and covers it with a little terracotta lid while it cooks.

"Mum or Dad always watches to make sure I don't burn myself, but I am really good at cooking eggs and I never do."

Dinner always includes a big bowl of rice. Khun Yai used to cook it in a clay pot, but now she has an electric rice cooker. Tonight there are six other dishes, including several different vegetables. AA eats lots of rice, but she says the vegetables are too spicy.

21

A special day in AA's life — a day out with Dad

Today is Saturday and AA is excited because she is going to spend the whole day with her father, Kittima. They set off on their bicycles, riding around the park near the temple. It is a peaceful place, away from the noise and traffic fumes of the city centre.

They stop at a stall selling drinks and ices made from fruit syrups. AA chooses strawberry-flavoured crushed ice with a topping of icing sugar. The ice melts quickly in the sun and AA sucks up the cold, sweet liquid with her straw.

"Next time I'll have durian ice cream. The fruit smells funny but the ice cream tastes good!"

AA and her family are friends with the Thai-Chinese family who run the local noodle shop. There are three types of noodles to choose from, with different sauces and toppings. Kittima has flat noodles with slices of cuttlefish, spring onions and chilli sauce. AA likes the thin noodles in soup. She doesn't want her day out with Dad to end, but they have fun planning the route they will take on their cycle ride home.

23

FRANCE

Jordan Pignier is eight years old. He lives in a village called St Gervais, in the Limousin region of Southwest France.

Jordan's father and mother, Jean Marc and Geneviéve, own a bar and restaurant. People come for breakfast, lunch and dinner, as well as in between for drinks and snacks. Jordan often works in the kitchen with his father and helps his mother look after the guests.

"My favourite things to eat are beef-burgers, steak, chips, chicken, garlic bread and chocolate cake — oh, and oysters."

At weekends, Jordan loves climbing trees in the forests outside his village. He usually says hello to a herd of Limousin cattle on the way. People visit Limousin from all over the world to enjoy good cooking and beautiful countryside.

After he gets up, Jordan comes downstairs to have breakfast in the bar. He dips his pain au chocolat, or some baguette with chocolate spread, into hot chocolate served in a special breakfast bowl. He finishes his drink quickly so that he'll be in time for the school bus when it stops outside the restaurant.

"I get up late and rush my breakfast on school days, but at weekends I wake up early so there is more day for me!"

School lunch today is vegetable soup, then turkey with peas and carrots, then fruit and cheese. The children have a different three-course meal every day. Breakfast is always a light meal in France, so lunch is important and Jordan is hungry. Today he eats the soup and the turkey, but he thinks the peas and carrots are too mushy. Jordan likes his father's cooking much better. He also prefers to eat at home because it's not so noisy!

25

When he has finished his homework, Jordan makes a chocolate cake. He doesn't need a recipe. He breaks eggs into a bowl, adds milk, chocolate powder, yoghurt, flour and butter, then tastes to check. He thinks the mixture needs more sugar. Once he is sure it's perfect, he butters a baking tin and puts the cake into the oven.

"When I grow up,
I might be a fireman,
a doctor or a chef."

While his cake is baking, Jordan helps prepare for dinner in the restaurant. He slices the baguettes with a special machine and carries a basket of bread to each table. Everyone eats lots of bread so the baskets are refilled throughout the evening.

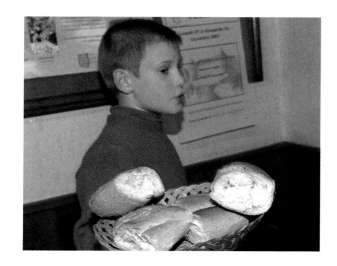

Before the guests arrive, the family has their own dinner. Jordan likes oysters because they taste of the sea. He enjoys cutting the oyster from its shell and scooping it into his mouth. His father has opened twelve for each of them.

"Oysters are good for you!"

A special day in Jordan's life – mushrooming

Early on Saturday mornings in the autumn, Jordan and his father Jean Marc go hunting for mushrooms. Each time they go, Jordan learns a bit more about the different types and how to tell them apart. He knows that there are some you shouldn't pick because they are poisonous.

"I started looking for mushrooms when I was young – I don't remember when."

The best mushrooms they find are called ceps. Some of them are as big as plates. Jordan is very pleased when he finds three large and two small ones.

Jordan is learning how to clean the mushroom stem by stripping the outer skin with a knife. He puts the pieces of mushroom that he cuts off back on the ground and covers them with moss so that they will grow into new mushrooms next year.

Back at home, Jean Marc cooks the mushrooms in butter. Jordan has some for dinner with steak and potatoes. He is proud that, thanks to him, the restaurant guests will enjoy a special treat tonight.

"We have been to mushroom paradise!"

INDIA

Yamini Arora lives with her parents, sister and grandparents in Kolkata, one of India's biggest cities. It used to be called Calcutta when this part of India was ruled by Britain. Yamini and her older sister, Soheni, are named after ragas, which are forms of Indian classical music.

From her home in a tall apartment block, Yamini can see the Hugli river that runs through the centre of the city. Lots of people take the ferry across the river every day to go to work. The Howrah bridge, which was made in the United Kingdom, is a famous landmark.

Yamini's grandmother, who she calls Amijee, helps to cook and care for the family. Yamini adores Amijee and loves to spend time shopping and cooking with her. As soon as she wakes up she goes to find Amijee for a cuddle.

Yamini has a light breakfast because school starts very early in the morning. She drinks a big mug of milk with a few biscuits, which she likes to share with her grandfather, Dadu. Some days she eats a bowl of chocolate flakes. At weekends, when there is more time, she has toast and sometimes an egg.

On the way to school with her mother, Yamini sees a street trader selling guavas, and stops to buy one. She will eat it for tiffin – her snack at school break. Yamini likes to eat fruit every day, especially mangoes and watermelon in summer. In winter, she has guavas, bananas, papaya, apples, oranges or berries.

"Today for tiffin, I've got popcorn, cucumber and guava and a biscuit. Sometimes I don't like my tiffin and I give it to the birds."

When school is over, Yamini and her sister come home for lunch. Yamini chops carrots to eat raw with cucumber. She is not allowed to fry the puris, a kind of puffed bread, as the oil is too hot. She can't wait for them to be ready. Yamini likes to eat puris with chutney and dal, a sauce made from lentils. After lunch she cooks a coconut sweet called naryal ladoo.

Yamini enjoys shopping for food in the market. It's called New Market, although it's in one of the city's oldest buildings. Before she goes inside, Yamini chooses vegetables from a street trader's stall for her favourite dish, aloo paratha – flat bread filled with potatoes and onion.

"Once I saw a chicken killed at the market.
The man pulled a chicken with black feathers
out of his basket, then he chopped off its head."

The grocery stall sells dried lentils and chickpeas for dal, colourful spices and several different kinds of rice. Yamini likes the delicate flavour of basmati. Today is Tuesday, vegetarian day for the whole family. For dinner they have rice, chapatis (flat bread), chickpea dal, vegetables and paneer, which is like cottage cheese. It's past nine o'clock when dinner is over, and Yamini is ready for bed.

A special day in Yamini's life — her birthday

On her seventh birthday, Yamini's mother gives her a soft toy cat. Yamini names it Hibiscus, after the red trumpet-shaped flowers in the roof garden of their apartment block. Then her sister helps her to pack a picnic. Yamini chooses her favourite snacks – cottage cheese sandwiches, biscuits and pineapple. Amijee has also made halwa, a special sweet with almonds that she makes for everyone's birthday.

"I always have a cake with candles, and jelly, and fryums – deep fried soya beans coloured red, blue, green and yellow."

Yamini and her mother enjoy the sunshine in the park before their picnic. Then they unpack the halwa from its decorated box and Yamini pours homemade lemon squash. Her mother makes it by squeezing lemons and adding sugar to the juice. She leaves the mixture in the sun until the sugar dissolves.

Yamini is looking forward to joining in the preparations for her birthday dinner. Amijee is making a cake, biscuits and jelly-jujus (jelly sweets covered in sugar). On the way home, they stop at Yamini's favourite cookie shop and her mother lets her choose whatever she wants. Yamini gets a cake for her grandfather, too. He likes sweet treats as much as she does!

RECIPES

Why not try out some of the children's favourite dishes for yourself?
You can buy all the ingredients you need from your local supermarket.
But remember to ask an adult for help before using the oven,
a hot pan or a knife.

Thembe's Condensed Milk Pudding

This is a kind of custard tart – called 'melktert' in South Africa. Thembe's version of melktert doesn't need baking. It's quite sweet, which is why she likes it.

1 packet of plain butter biscuits
1 tin of condensed milk
750ml warm water
15g butter or margarine
60g cornflour
75ml cold water
1 teaspoon vanilla essence
2 medium eggs
cinnamon (optional)

Put a few biscuits to one side and arrange the rest in an overlapping layer in the bottom of a dish. Put the butter or margarine into a saucepan with the condensed milk and water, and stir over a low heat until smooth.

In a separate bowl, mix the cornflour, cold water, vanilla essence and eggs. Then add this mixture to the saucepan and cook gently for about ten minutes.

Slowly pour the mixture over the biscuit base. Crush your leftover biscuits and scatter the crumbs over the top. Add a dusting of powdered cinnamon if you like.

Put the tart in the fridge to set for a couple of hours before eating.

Luis' Tomato Salsa

You could try this delicious tomato relish with chips or fish fingers, or with burgers and sausages at a barbecue. It would be especially good as a dip with tortilla crisps or pitta bread.

4 large or 6 medium-sized ripe tomatoes • 2 red onions • a bunch of fresh coriander
2 green chilli peppers • 1 teaspoon sugar • a pinch or two of salt • a lemon

Finely chop the tomatoes and onions and mix together in a bowl. Roughly chop the coriander leaves and add. Cut open the two chillis and scrape out the seeds – wash your hands straight after doing this as they can sting. Finely slice the deseeded chillis and mix with the other ingredients, along with the sugar, salt and a sprinkle of lemon juice. Leave your salsa to stand for a while before eating so that the flavours have time to combine.

You don't need to stick to exact quantities for this recipe. You might find you prefer more or less salt, or lemon juice – it's up to you. A little sugar helps to bring out the taste of tomatoes. And if you don't like chilli, just leave it out!

AA's Thai Fried Eggs

AA eats her favourite fried eggs with rice, but they would taste just as good with bread or chips – or perhaps some bacon.

2 large eggs • 2 spring onions
1 tablespoon fish sauce (from the supermarket or an Asian grocery store)
1 tablespoon soy sauce • 1 tablespoon water
1 tablespoon vegetable or sunflower oil
fresh coriander leaves (optional)

Whisk the eggs with the fish sauce, soy sauce and water. Finely chop the spring onions and add to the egg mixture. Then heat the oil in a frying pan or wok until very hot. Tip in the egg mixture, lifting the egg so that it cooks evenly. When it begins to brown underneath, flip it over with a spatula and cook the other side. Slide on to a flat plate and garnish with coriander.

Jordan's Chocolate Cake

Jordan makes this cake without a recipe because he has made it lots of times before. The unusual ingredient is yoghurt, which makes the cake moist and light. You could use buttermilk instead. Remember to ask an adult to put the cake into the oven and take it out. It tastes delicious with vanilla ice cream, or spread with cream cheese.

250g plain flour
1 tablespoon baking powder
1 teaspoon bicarbonate of soda
200g softened butter
200g sugar
2 eggs
2 teaspoons vanilla essence
70g cocoa powder
250ml natural yoghurt

Preheat the oven to 180°C / 350°F / Gas Mark 4.

Lightly grease a 20cm, round cake tin. Sieve flour, baking powder and bicarbonate of soda into a bowl and put aside. In another bowl, cream together the butter and sugar. Add the eggs and vanilla essence and beat lightly until combined. Sprinkle in the cocoa, then pour in the yoghurt and mix well. Add the flour from your other bowl and fold in lightly.

Spoon the mixture into the greased tin and smooth the top. Bake for one hour, until a metal skewer (or knife) inserted into the middle of the cake comes out clean. Don't worry if the top of the cake is cracked.

Let the cake cool for a while in its tin, before turning out on to a wire rack.

Yamini's Coconut Sweet

In Hindi, the language Yamini speaks, this recipe is called 'naryal ladoo' ('naryal' means 'coconut'). Naryal ladoo is very easy to make – Yamini makes it after lunch and eats it straightaway.

To try naryal ladoo for yourself, you'll need to buy a fresh coconut from a supermarket, greengrocer or street market. Ask an adult to break it open for you, and pour the cloudy coconut milk into a jug. It's good to drink, or you can add it to a curry.

Cardamom is a fragrant spice, used a lot in Indian cooking; you can find it on the spice shelves at the supermarket.

1 large coconut
200g sugar
½ teaspoon ground cardamom

Once you have poured the milk from your coconut, ask an adult to chop it into chunks for you. Using a coarse grater, next grate the white flesh into a bowl. Then put the sugar into a frying pan or wok and heat it until it starts to melt. Add the grated coconut and cardamom and stir until the mixture starts sticking together and goes a light golden-brown colour. Turn off the heat at this point, but keep stirring until the mixture is cool enough to handle.

Take small pieces of the mixture and roll them into balls about the size of a walnut. Put them on a plate and leave them to cool completely before eating.

Food Glossary

South Africa

amasi Milk left to curdle and go sour. Many Zulu people prefer amasi to fresh milk.

condensed milk Thickened, sweetened milk, sold in tins.

maize Another word for corn: long white or yellow spears of grain which grow inside tall, leafy plants. Maize is a staple food in South Africa (which means it is eaten every day).

mealie meal A rough, white flour made from ground maize. It is cooked to make puthu, which is very filling and cheaper than rice or potatoes.

umoba Sugar cane, a tall grass that is grown as a crop. The sweet syrup inside the cane is extracted to make sugar.

Mexico

coriander A herb that looks similar to parsley, but with a spicy smell and flavour. The leaves and seeds are used in cooking.

corn The American word for maize. The spears of grain can be eaten whole as 'corn on the cob', or ground to make flour.

fried beans Dried beans, first cooked in water, then fried and mashed.

rice pudding Rice cooked with sugar and milk, sometimes spiced with cinnamon or nutmeg.

sweet bread Light bread, like cake, eaten for breakfast or snacks.

tortillas Thin, flat pancakes made from corn, eaten at nearly every meal in Mexico.

Thailand

cuttlefish A sea creature like a squid, but with a broader body. Like squid, cuttlefish produce dark brown ink, which is used in cooking as well as the body and tentacles.

durian fruit A large, spiky tropical fruit with green skin. The creamy flesh inside smells rotten but has a fresh taste.

noodles Thin, long strips of pasta, usually served in soup or stir fried.

quails' eggs The delicate-flavoured eggs laid by quails. Quails are small, short-tailed game birds, and are also good to eat.

rice The main crop of Asia, grown in flooded fields called paddies. Rice is a type of grass; the grains of rice grow inside the seeds.

soy sauce A salty brown sauce made from soya beans.

France

baguette A long, crusty white loaf of bread. French people buy them fresh every day.

cep A large wild mushroom with white flesh and a rich, woody taste.

garlic bread Bread spread with butter mixed with garlic, then heated in the oven.

oysters Flat, round shells found on the sea bed, each containing a morsel of sea-tasting flesh.

pain au chocolat A sweet breakfast pastry, like a croissant, filled with melted chocolate.

India

basmati rice A small, long-grained rice with a nutty flavour and smell.

chapati Round, flat bread made of wheat flour and water. Chapatis are often used to scoop up dal and other sauces.

dal Pulses such as lentils or chickpeas cooked with spices and served as a sauce or a soup.

guava A round, yellow-skinned tropical fruit with a strong, sweet smell and pink flesh.

papaya A large, pear-shaped tropical fruit with a bright yellow skin and smooth yellow flesh.

Index

MORE TITLES IN PAPERBACK
FROM FRANCES LINCOLN

WAKE UP, WORLD!
Beatrice Hollyer
Introduction by Tony Robinson
In association with Oxfam

Explore the lives of eight children from different countries around the world.
We look inside their homes and meet their families; they tell us about their schools,
how they help out at home and what makes their day fun.
This is a celebration of the diversity of our world,
and a tribute to the children who live in it.
ISBN 0-7112-1484-0

WE ARE BRITAIN!
Poems by Benjamin Zephaniah
Photographs by Prodeepta Das

From cutting-edge performance poet, Benjamin Zephaniah, comes a collection of poems
about thirteen children from all over Britain. The children have a wide range
of cultural backgrounds, likes and dislikes. This is the rhyming, rapping,
rhythmic way to learn about Britain in the 21st Century.
ISBN 0-7112-1902-8

SAYING GOODBYE:
A SPECIAL FAREWELL TO MAMA NKWELLE
Ifeoma Onyefulu

A little boy called Ikenna describes the ceremonial goodbye
given to his great-grandmother after her burial. Ifeoma Onyefulu's
sensitive text and photographs give fascinating insights
into the funeral customs of an Igbo village.
ISBN 0-7112-1701-7

Frances Lincoln titles are available from all good bookshops.
You can also buy books and find out more about your favourite titles,
authors and illustrators on our website: www.franceslincoln.com.